THE WHITE HOUSE

Author: Holly Karapetkova

Rourke
Publishing LLC
Vero Beach, Florida 32964

www.rourkepublishing.com

PHOTO CREDITS: © Kalim: page 5; © Library of Congress: page 7, 8, 10, 13, 19, 21, 23, 24, 27; © Wikipedia.com: page 8; © Royce DeGrie: page 9; © Sarfa: page 13; © DHuss: page 15; © Wikipedia.com: page 25, 26; © mistydawnphoto: page 25; © Glenda M. Powers: page 29

Editor: Jeanne Sturm

Cover Design: Nicola Stratford: bdpublishing.com

Page Design: Renee Brady

Library of Congress Cataloging-in-Publication Data

Karapetkova, Holly.
  The White House / Holly Karapetkova.
    p. cm. -- (American symbols and landmarks)
  ISBN 978-1-60472-346-5 (Hardcover)
  ISBN 978-1-60472-976-4 (Softcover)
  1. White House (Washington, D.C.)--Juvenile literature.
  F204.W5 K365 2009
  975.3 22
                                2008007736

Printed in the USA

IG/IG

Rourke Publishing

www.rourkepublishing.com – rourke@rourkepublishing.com
Post Office Box 3328, Vero Beach, FL 32964

Table of Contents

The White House: An American Ideal

The White House sits in Washington, D. C., the nation's capital. It is the building where the president of the United States of America has worked and lived for over 200 years. But for many people in America and around the world, the White House is more than just a building. It represents an ideal: it is a symbol of the freedom and democracy that are a part of American government.

The White House symbolizes the president, the leader of the United States and the head of the **executive branch** of government. It is also a symbol of our nation's past, reflecting two centuries of American history. Indeed, it is hard to imagine a building more important to our nation than the White House.

The President's House: Two Hundred Years

George Washington, America's first president, helped plan the White House while he was in office. He held a contest to see who could come up with the best design for the building. James Hoban, an architect who was born in Ireland and who lived in Charleston, South Carolina, won the contest. In 1792, construction of the house began with James Hoban in charge.

Building the house was not an easy task. Some craftsmen and workers were brought from Europe, but many of the builders were African-American slaves and freemen. They worked long hours, sometimes seven days a week, and completed the house in eight years.

The first president to live in the house was John Adams, the second president of the United States. When he and his wife moved in, the large house didn't have much furniture. It was so empty, in fact, that the First Lady used the East Room to hang out her laundry!

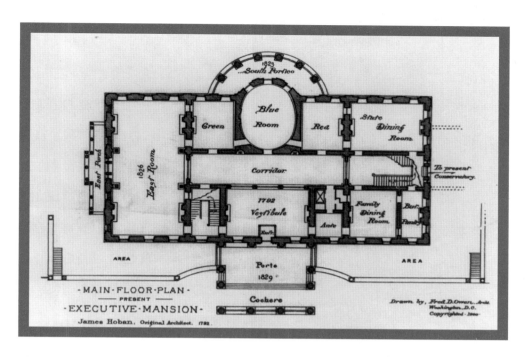

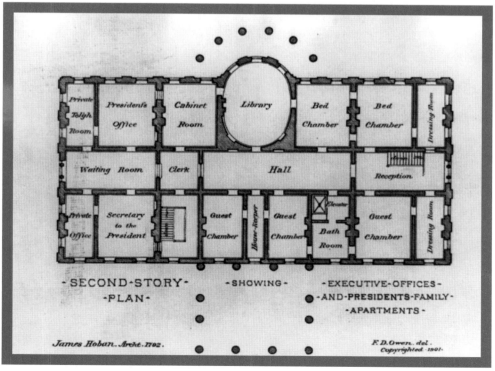

James Hoban's design for the White House was selected
from among nine architects' plans.

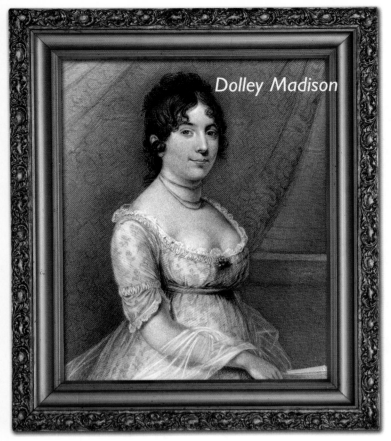
Dolley Madison

During the War of 1812, the British set the White House on fire. Dolley Madison, the First Lady, saved a famous portrait of George Washington, the Declaration of Independence, and some other important documents. But the rest of the house was destroyed; only the outside walls were left standing.

President Madison decided to rebuild the house exactly as it had been before. With the help of the original architect, James Hoban, and some of the original builders, the White House was rebuilt.

This portrait of George Washington was done by Gilbert Stuart in 1797.

We the People

of the United States, in order to form a more perfect Union, establish Justice, insure domestic Tranquility, provide for the common defence, promote the general Welfare, and secure the Blessings of Liberty to ourselves and our Posterity, do ordain and establish this Constitution for the United States of America.

Article. I.

Section. 1. All legislative Powers herein granted shall be vested in a Congress of the United States, which shall consist of a Senate and House of Representatives.

Section. 2. The House of Representatives shall be composed of Members chosen every second Year by the People of the several States, and the Electors in each State shall have the Qualifications requisite for Electors of the most numerous Branch of the State Legislature.

No Person shall be a Representative who shall not have attained to the Age of twenty five Years, and been seven Years a Citizen of the United States, and who shall not, when elected, be an Inhabitant of that State in which he shall be chosen.

Representatives and direct Taxes shall be apportioned among the several States which may be included within this Union, according to their respective Numbers, which shall be determined by adding to the whole Number of free Persons, including those bound to Service for a Term of Years, and excluding Indians not taxed, three fifths of all other Persons. The actual Enumeration shall be made within three Years after the first Meeting of the Congress of the United States, and within every subsequent Term of ten Years, in such Manner as they shall by Law direct. The Number of Representatives shall not exceed one for every thirty Thousand, but each State shall have at Least one Representative; and until such enumeration shall be made, the State of New Hampshire shall be entitled to chuse three, Massachusetts eight, Rhode Island and Providence Plantations one, Connecticut five, New York six, New Jersey four, Pennsylvania eight, Delaware one, Maryland six, Virginia ten, North Carolina five, South Carolina five, and Georgia three.

When vacancies happen in the Representation from any State, the Executive Authority thereof shall issue Writs of Election to fill such Vacancies.

The House of Representatives shall chuse their Speaker and other Officers; and shall have the sole Power of Impeachment.

Section. 3. The Senate of the United States shall be composed of two Senators from each State, chosen by the Legislature thereof, for six Years; and each Senator shall have one Vote.

Immediately after they shall be assembled in Consequence of the first Election, they shall be divided as equally as may be into three Classes. The Seats of the Senators of the first Class shall be vacated at the Expiration of the second Year, of the second Class at the Expiration of the fourth Year, and of the third Class at the Expiration of the sixth Year, so that one third may be chosen every second Year; and if Vacancies happen by Resignation, or otherwise, during the Recess of the Legislature of any State, the Executive thereof may make temporary Appointments until the next Meeting of the Legislature, which shall then fill such Vacancies.

No Person shall be a Senator who shall not have attained to the Age of thirty Years, and been nine Years a Citizen of the United States, and who shall not, when elected, be an Inhabitant of that State for which he shall be chosen.

The Vice President of the United States shall be President of the Senate, but shall have no Vote, unless they be equally divided.

The Senate shall chuse their other Officers, and also a President pro tempore, in the Absence of the Vice President, or when he shall exercise the Office of President of the United States.

The Senate shall have the sole Power to try all Impeachments. When sitting for that Purpose, they shall be on Oath or Affirmation. When the President of the United States is tried, the Chief Justice shall preside: And no Person shall be convicted without the Concurrence of two thirds of the Members present.

Judgment in Cases of Impeachment shall not extend further than to removal from Office, and disqualification to hold and enjoy any Office of honor, Trust or Profit under the United States: but the Party convicted shall nevertheless be liable and subject to Indictment, Trial, Judgment and Punishment, according to Law.

Section. 4. The Times, Places and Manner of holding Elections for Senators and Representatives, shall be prescribed in each State by the Legislature thereof; but the Congress may at any time by Law make or alter such Regulations, except as to the Places of chusing Senators.

The Congress shall assemble at least once in every Year, and such Meeting shall be on the first Monday in December, unless they shall by Law appoint a different Day.

Section. 5. Each House shall be the Judge of the Elections, Returns and Qualifications of its own Members, and a Majority of each shall constitute a Quorum to do Business; but a smaller Number may adjourn from day to day, and may be authorized to compel the Attendance of absent Members, in such Manner, and under such Penalties as each House may provide.

Each House may determine the Rules of its Proceedings, punish its Members for disorderly Behaviour, and, with the Concurrence of two thirds, expel a Member.

Each House shall keep a Journal of its Proceedings, and from time to time publish the same, excepting such Parts as may in their Judgment require Secrecy; and the Yeas and Nays of the Members of either House on any question shall, at the Desire of one fifth of those Present, be entered on the Journal.

Neither House, during the Session of Congress, shall, without the Consent of the other, adjourn for more than three days, nor to any other Place than that in which the two Houses shall be sitting.

Section. 6. The Senators and Representatives shall receive a Compensation for their Services, to be ascertained by Law, and paid out of the Treasury of the United States. They shall in all Cases, except Treason, Felony and Breach of the Peace, be privileged from Arrest during their Attendance at the Session of their respective Houses, and in going to and returning from the same; and for any Speech or Debate in either House, they shall not be questioned in any other Place.

No Senator or Representative shall, during the Time for which he was elected, be appointed to any civil Office under the Authority of the United States, which shall have been created, or the Emoluments whereof shall have been encreased during such time; and no Person holding any Office under the United States, shall be a Member of either House during his Continuance in Office.

Section 7. All Bills for raising Revenue shall originate in the House of Representatives; but the Senate may propose or concur with Amendments as on other Bills.

Every Bill which shall have passed the House of Representatives and the Senate, shall, before it become a Law, be presented to the President of the

The Declaration of Independence

Over the next few years, the house was updated in important ways. In 1833, President Andrew Jackson had running water installed. In 1840, President Martin Van Buren had a heating system put in.

The first telephone was connected in 1879, and electric wiring was installed in 1891 by President Benjamin Harrison.

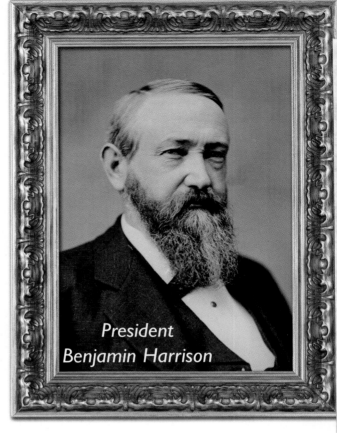

President Benjamin Harrison

He and his wife were afraid of being shocked by the new electric system and had servants turn on the lights for them!

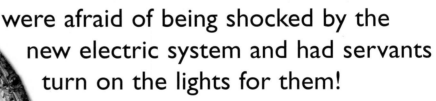

Caroline Harrison was First Lady from 1889 to 1893.

Did you know?

When the White House was first built, it wasn't called the White House. Its official name was the Executive Mansion, *but most people called it the President's House. However, it was white. The original builders* **whitewashed** *the house in order to protect the* **sandstone** *blocks on the outer walls. Because this whitewash made the house look white,* people started to use the nickname White House. In 1901, President Theodore Roosevelt made it the house's official name.

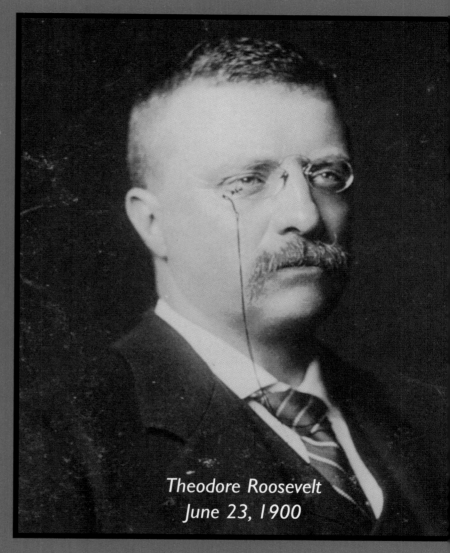

Theodore Roosevelt
June 23, 1900

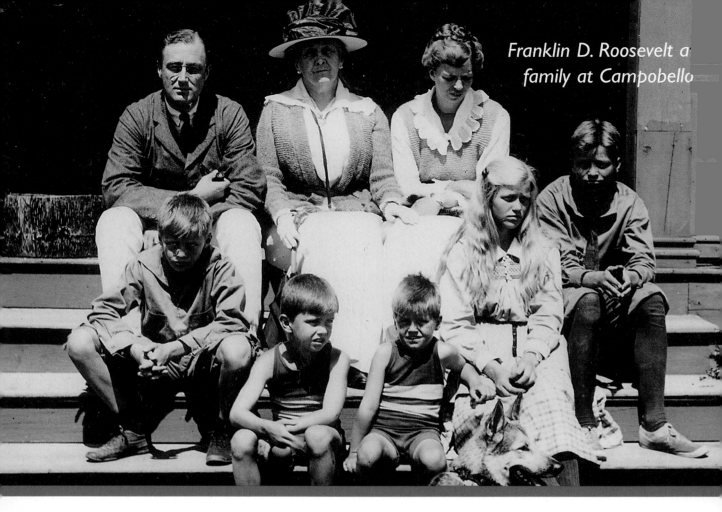

Franklin D. Roosevelt a[nd] family at Campobello

In 1901, President Theodore Roosevelt moved into the White House with his six children and their many pets. Not surprisingly, they found the living space of the White House too small. So in 1902 the West **Wing** was added as a working space for the president and his staff. The family was then able to use the old offices as part of their living area.

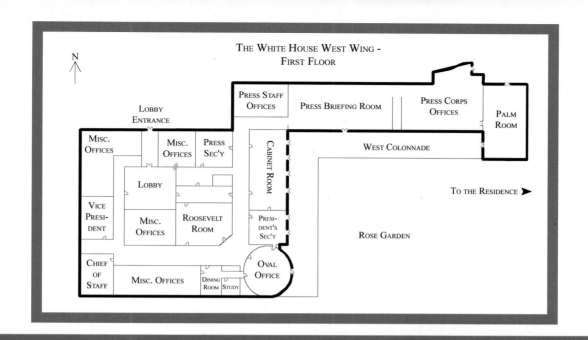

THE WHITE HOUSE WEST WING -
FIRST FLOOR

N

PRESS STAFF OFFICES

PRESS BRIEFING ROOM

PRESS CORPS OFFICES

PALM ROOM

LOBBY ENTRANCE

MISC. OFFICES

MISC. OFFICES

PRESS SEC'Y

CABINET ROOM

WEST COLONNADE

LOBBY

TO THE RESIDENCE ➤

VICE PRESI-DENT

MISC. OFFICES

ROOSEVELT ROOM

PRESI-DENT'S SEC'Y

ROSE GARDEN

CHIEF OF STAFF

MISC. OFFICES

DINING ROOM

STUDY

OVAL OFFICE

Fun Fact!

Our heaviest president, President William Howard Taft, weighed more than 300 pounds. The bathtubs in the White House were too narrow, and he kept getting stuck in them. He had workers install a huge tub that held almost 65 gallons (246 liters) of water. It was big enough for all four of the workers to sit in it at once!

A Tour of the White House

The White House has 132 rooms. Some of these rooms are used for the business of running the country. Some are used for holding government functions and entertaining important guests. Still others are part of the first family's private living space.

The Red Room has traditionally been used as a sitting room and has sometimes hosted small dinner parties.

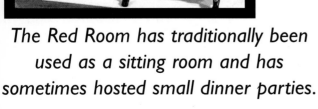

The Green Room has served as a dining room, a card room, and a sitting room over the past two hundred years.

The First Floor

East Room

The first floor contains several famous rooms. The East Room has been used for many different types of events over the years, from weddings and concerts to press conferences and bill-signing ceremonies. It even served as a camp for soldiers during the Civil War.

The Blue Room, which is at the center of the first floor, is oval-shaped. The President often greets **diplomats** and other important guests in this room.

In the State Dining Room, official White House **banquets** and other events are held.

16

Eisenhower and other presidents have held many parties in the East Room.

Blue Room

President Barack Obama and First Lady, Michelle Obama, greet members of the public in the Blue Room.

The Second and Third Floors

The second and third Floors are reserved for the First Family's private life. They contain many bedrooms, the most famous of which is the Lincoln Bedroom.

Abraham Lincoln used this room as an office while he was president. Several First Family members and guests have reported seeing Lincoln's ghost in this room!

Lincoln Bedroom

The family living quarters also include several sitting rooms (including the lovely Yellow Oval Room), a dining area, and a kitchen.

Yellow Oval Room

Family Dining Area

The White House North Lawn during Lincoln's administration (1861-65)

The West Wing

The president and his staff work in the West Wing. In one corner of the West Wing sits the president's office, or Oval Office. For many Americans, the Oval Office represents the leadership and power of the president. While this room is not open to the public, the president often invites Americans into the Oval Office via television, and many presidents have given important speeches in this office.

Did you know?

The Oval Office and the other oval-shaped rooms in the White House have a very unusual shape. When our first president, George Washington, was in office, he would have guests gather around in a circle. He would stand in the center and walk around the circle, greeting each guest personally. Because of the way President Washington greeted his guests, he liked his rooms to be round. The oval-shaped rooms in the White House come from his design.

President George Bush meets with president-elect Barack Obama, November 10, 2008.

Oval Office

First Families

Many presidents have lived in the White House with their families over the past two centuries. Some of these presidents have had large families, with many children and grandchildren. President Franklin Roosevelt had 13 grandchildren, and President John Tyler had 15 children, though only four lived in the White House.

President Abraham Lincoln had three sons. When he first entered office, Robert was 17 years old, Willie was 10, and Tad was 7. Tad had a lot of fun in the White House. He had two pet goats that wandered freely around the house. He once tied them to a chair and had them pull him around!

The time in the White House wasn't all fun and games for the Lincolns, though. When Willie was only 11 years old he died of a fever, and the family never fully recovered from his death.

President Lincoln reads a boo *with his son Tad.*

Theodore Roosevelt's family was very large. He had six children, two girls and four boys. They were a rowdy

bunch. They threw spitballs at a painting of Andrew Jackson. They roller skated down the hallways and slid down the stairs on trays. Once, when Archie Roosevelt was sick and stuck inside, his younger brother Quentin took Archie's pony, Algonquin, up on the elevator to Archie's bedroom. President Roosevelt wrote, "I don't think that any family has ever enjoyed the White House more than we have," and he was probably right.

Quentin and the other Roosevelt children brought ponies, dogs, sheep, and many other pets with them to the White House.

24

President John F. Kennedy entered the White House in 1961 with two small children, Caroline and John, Jr. They played in the house as they grew up. Caroline even went to first grade in the White House with ten of her friends. Her mother arranged a classroom on the third floor.

John Jr., Jacqueline, Caroline, and John F. Kennedy pose for a family photo in 1962.

President Carter's daughter Amy, President Clinton's daughter Chelsea, and President George W. Bush's twin daughters, Jenna and Barbara, have also spent much of their lives in the spotlight growing up in the White House.

Shortly after they moved in, a swing set was erected on the White House lawn for Malia and Sasha Obama.

Who Works at the White House?

It takes a huge staff to keep the White House running smoothly. Around 100 men and women work at the White House, taking care of the cooking, cleaning, and even the grocery shopping.

Perhaps the most important member of the White House staff is the Chief Usher. The Chief Usher works as a general manager, watching over the entire house and its staff. Although presidents change every four or eight years, many of the White House workers like the Chief Usher stay the same. They are very proud to serve America's leader, whoever it may be at the time.

This photo shows an overhead view of the White House Grounds.

Slavery in the White House

Some of the early presidents like Thomas Jefferson, James Madison, and Andrew Jackson brought their slaves to work in the White House. When Abraham Lincoln became president, he refused to use slave labor. On January 1, 1863, he signed the **Emancipation Proclamation**, giving all slaves their freedom and making sure that no slaves would ever work at the White House again. This was a great day for America.

President Andrew Jackson was the seventh president of the United States.

The People's House

Most presidents feel when they enter the White House that they are only temporary caretakers of a home that truly belongs to the people of the United States. From the beginning, the White House has been thought of as America's house, and this is part of what makes it so special. From 1801 to 1932, the White House was open for a public **reception** every New Year's Day. Everyone was welcome, and at times there were up to 6,000 people waiting in line to visit.

While today's presidents don't hold public receptions, the White House is still the only home of a world leader that is open to the people.

Diagram of
the White House

WEST COLONNADE

EXECUTIVE
RESIDENCE

EAST COLONNADE

WEST WING

ROSE GARDEN

JACQUELINE
KENNEDY
GARDEN

EAST WING

29

White House Facts

How big is your home? How many bathrooms do you have? How many windows? Here are some facts about the White House:

Length: 168 feet (51 meters)
Width: 85 .5 feet (26 meters)
Height: 70 feet (21 meters)
Gallons of paint it takes to cover the exterior of the center (not including the East and West Wings): 300 gallons (1,136 liters)
Total area of the grounds: 18 acres (7 hectares)
Total area inside the house: 55,000 square feet (5,110 square meters)
Total number of presidents who have lived at the White House with their families: 41

Total number of rooms in the White House: 132
There are:
35 bathrooms
40 hallways
11 bedrooms
28 fireplaces
4 kitchens
5 elevators
17 closets
412 doors
147 windows

Visiting the White House
You can schedule a tour of the White House through your member of Congress up to six months in advance. You can find your member of Congress online at www.senate.gov or www.house.gov.

Glossary

banquets (BANG-kwitz): formal dinners given in honor of a person or an occasion

diplomats (DIP-luh-matz): officials who work with other nations and governments to reach agreements

emancipation (i-man-si-PAY-shun): the state of being freed from someone else's power, as in being freed from slavery

executive branch (eg-ZEK-yuh-tiv BRANCH): one of the three branches of American government that executes (or puts into action) laws passed by the Congress (the Legislative Branch)

proclamation (prok-luh-MAY-shun): something that is publicly announced

reception (ree-SEP-shun): a social gathering where guests are received

sandstone (SAND-stohn): a rock that is made of sand and held together by natural cement

whitewashed (WITE-woshd): covered in a thin white paint

Wing (WING): part of the building that sticks out from the central or main part

Further Reading

Grace, Catherine O'Neill. *The White House: An Illustrated History*. Scholastic, 2003.

Karr, Kathleen. *It Happened in the White House: Extraordinary Tales from America's Most Famous Home*. Hyperion Books for Children, 2000.

Truman, Margaret. *The President's House: 1800 to the Present: The Secrets and History of the World's Most Famous Home*. Ballantine Books, 2005.

Index

Websites

www.whitehouse.gov

www.whitehouse.gov/kids/White House

www.whitehousehistory.org

You can email the president at: president@whitehouse.gov

About the Author

Holly Karapetkova, Ph.D, loves writing poems and books for kids and adults. She teaches at Marymount University and lives in the Washington, D.C., area with her husband, her son K.J., and her two dogs, Muffy and Attila.